Canon EOS Reb

The Most Complete Step by
EOS Rebel T7/2000D Came ~puates with Useful
Photography Tips & Tricks for Beginners

Perry

Hoover

Disclaimer

The information in this book is based on personal experience and anecdotal evidence. Although the author has made every attempt to achieve an accuracy of the information gathered in this book, they make no representation or warranties concerning the accuracy or completeness of the contents of this book. Your circumstances may not be suited to some illustrations in this book.

The author disclaims any liability arising directly or indirectly from the use of this book. Readers are encouraged to seek Medical. Accounting, legal, or professional help when required.

This guide is for informational purposes only, and the author does not accept any responsibilities for any liabilities resulting from the use of this information. While every attempt has been made to verify the information provided here, the author cannot assume any responsibility for errors, inaccuracies or omission.

Printed in the United States of America

Table of Contents

INTRODUCTION...i

CHAPTER ONE 1

About Canon Rebel.. 1

   Specifications 1

   Other Camera Features 1

   Camera Design 2

   Equipment Accessories.. 5

   Features.. 6

   Extra Characteristics 12

CHAPTER TWO 17

Set Up your Device.. 17

   How to use the USB device to connect it to the
   Computer... 17

   How to connect Wi-Fi to send images 22

   How to remove Battery and Memory Card 28

   How the Battery can be Charged 29

CHAPTER THREE 33

The Process of Mounting the Lens.................................... 33

   How to Modify Diopter Correction 36

How to Turn the Camera On and Off 38

How to adjust the Time and Date Settings 39

CHAPTER FOUR 43

How to Insert a Secure Digital Memory Card 43

Exploring the Camera's External Feature 44

Front-left Control Features 56

Basic Camera Features and Settings 58

CHAPTER FIVE 61

How to Navigate the Custom Function Screens 61

How to Display the Camera Settings Screen................ 64

How to Use the Monitor as Viewfinder in Live View
Shooting 68

Adjusting the Shooting Settings Display 70

Viewfinder data reading 71

CHAPTER SIX 74

How to Change the Live View Display 74

How to Use the Quick Control Screen to modify settings
.... 77

Basic Setup Options Overview 81

How to Select an Exposure Mode 91

CHAPTER SEVEN 93

Basic Zone Modes... 93

Creative Zone Modes 95

How to Choose a Shutter-Release (Drive) Mode......... 96

Understanding the Drive Mode Options...................... 96

Self-timer Settings 99

How to Check and Modify the Drive Mode 101

Setting the Image Quality Setting............................ 102

CHAPTER EIGHT 106

Using the Camera Flash 106

How to Add Flash 106

How to Enable and Disable Flash 109

How to Use Flash with Red-Eye Reduction.............. 114

How to Modify Flash Power with Flash Exposure
Compensation... 116

How to Lock the Flash Exposure............................ 119

CHAPTER NINE 123

How to Scene Intelligent Auto Mode 123

Scene Intelligent Auto and Flash Off settings for
viewfinder photography.. 124

Scene Intelligent Auto and Flash Off settings for Live
View photography 129

Exposure Trio (Aperture, Shutter Speed, and ISO)...... 131

How the Depth of Field is Also Affected by Aperture 135

How Shutter Speed Affects Motion Blur 136

CHAPTER TEN 139

How ISO Affects Picture Noise 139

    Exposure Modes for Advanced Lighting (P, Tv, Av, and M) 140

    How to Monitor Exposure Settings................................ 143

    How to Choose a Metering Mode for Exposure......... 149

CHAPTER ELEVEN... 153

Camera Problems troubleshooting................................ 153

CONCLUSION 158

ABOUT THE AUTHOR 161

INTRODUCTION

The Canon Rebel T7 (known in Europe as the EOS 2000D) is effectively a 24-megapixel replacement for Canon's previous entry-level camera, the EOS 1300D. (Rebel T6). It is also a step up from Canon's much cheaper Rebel T100 (EOS 4000D), which is no longer available for purchase.

The Rebel T7/EOS 2000D features Canon's entry-level nine-point autofocus system, an ISO range of 100–6,400 (easily deployable to ISO 12,800), three frames per second of continuous shooting, and a non-articulating back screen.

NFC connectivity and Wi-Fi are available for wirelessly connecting to other devices. Even though its features are pretty simple by today's standards, the 2000D is a great way for beginners on a budget to get started with **"serious"** photography.

Like its predecessors, the Canon Rebel T7 EOS 2000D includes several settings for experienced photographers and a variety of tools to help beginners succeed. This Rebel offers several distinctive Wi-Fi functions, such as the capacity to wirelessly transmit pictures to a smartphone or tablet and use that gadget as a remote control for the camera.

CHAPTER ONE

About Canon Rebel

Specifications

Basic Camera Information

- Camera Brand   - Canon

- Camera Model   - EOS Rebel T7

- Camera Type - Digital SLR

Other Camera Features

- Burst Mode – Yes

- HDR Photography Mode – No

- Image Stabilization – No

- Type of Image Stabilization - N/A

- Equal Balance – Yes

Camera Design

- Dimension (H x W x D) - 101.3 x 129 x 77.6 mm

- Weight (g) -   475 g

- Color Choices - Black

- Body Components - Carbon fiber and polycarbonate composite material

Flash features

- Internal Flash – Yes

- Estimated Flash Range - Maximum coverage with a focal length of around 17mm (35mm equivalent: 28mm)

- Flash Management (Mode) - Auto E-TTL

Shutter Features

- Shutter type - Vertical-travel shutter with electrical first-curtain control and mechanical second-curtain control.

- Shutter Speed - 30-1/4000 seconds (in increments of 1/2 or 1/3 stop)

Focusing Features

- Autofocus Modes - AI Focus AF, Predictive AI Servo AF, and One-Shot AF

- Autofocus Zoom - EV 0 -18 at 23°C and ISO100 (AF Center), EV 1 -18 at 23°C and ISO100 (Other AF points)

- Automatic Type - TTL-CT-SIR equipped with a CMOS sensor.

- Manual Focus-Yes

Ports and Connectivity

- Wi-Fi - IEEE802.11b/g/n

- HDMI – Yes

- NFC – Yes

- Bluetooth – None

- USB - Yes

Sensor Features

- Sensor Size - 22.3 x 14.9 mm (APS-C)

- Sensor Type - 24.1 CMOS

- Effective Pixels - 24.1 megapixels

Sound Features

- Microphone – No

Display Features

- Type of Camera Display - LCD (TFT)

- Size of Camera Display - 75 mm

- Interactive Display – No

- Live Sample - Yes

Video Recording

- Supported Resolutions - Full HD (1920 x 1080) / HD (1280 x 720) / VGA (640 x 480)

- Slow-Motion Impact - N/A

Camera Storage

- Memory Card Format - SD, SDHC, SDXC

- Still Image file formats - JPEG, RAW

- Additional Storage file types - MOV MPEG4 AVC/H.264 video, Linear PCM audio

Power Source and Battery

- Power Source - AC Adapter Kit ACK-E10, Battery charger LC-E10, LC-E10E

- Battery Specifications - 1 x Lithium-ion Rechargeable Battery LP-E10

- Anticipated battery life - Viewfinder: Approximately 500 frames (23°C, AE 50%, FA 50%) / Approximately 410 frames (0°C, AE 50%, FA 50%). Live View: Approximately 240 shots (at 23°C, AE 50%, and FA 50%) / Approximately 230 shots (at 0°C, AE 50%, and FA 50%).

Equipment Accessories

- Lens Cap – No

- Lenses - Canon EF lenses

- Strap - Hand Strap E2

- USB Cord – No

- Camera Cover – No

- Different Accessories - LP-E10 battery pack, LC-E10 battery charger, GP-E2 GPS receiver, HDMI cable, and RS-60E3 remote switch.

Features

Build and Handling

The external controls are simple but functional. On the back of the EOS 2000D, there are buttons for white balance, ISO, drive mode, and autofocus settings. This makes it easy for advanced users to start experimenting with settings without having to dig through menus.

The autofocus is unsatisfactory. The sensor does not use Canon's Hybrid CMOS AF or Dual Pixel CMOS AF autofocus technology. This is likely acceptable for the camera's intended audience. This makes Live View focusing slow and jerky, especially since the kit lens that comes with the 2000D doesn't have

Canon's USM or STM autofocus actuators, which are quieter but probably cost more.

Durability

Even though the Rebel T6/T7 is an entry-level model, it does not feel cheap when held. The Rebel series is not as well-constructed as the *0D series, but these cameras nevertheless have a sturdy, high-quality feel, with a rubberized grip surface for the fingertips.

This camera's marketing will not boast about its magnesium alloy chassis or extreme weather sealing, but the T7's carbon fiber/glass fiber and polycarbonate resin construction should withstand typical use quite well.

Shutter life rating is also omitted from marketing materials, and an entry-level camera will invariably have a simple shutter system. It's uncommon for me to hear of an EOS shutter failing under normal conditions, and I doubt many T7 users will encounter this issue.

Viewfinder

DSLR viewfinders are superior to point-and-shoot camera viewfinders (if they even have one), however, the T7 viewfinder is diminutive in comparison to other DSLR viewfinders. Perceived viewfinder size is mostly dependent on familiarity, although the T7's compact body is accompanied by a similarly compact viewfinder. Compared to point-and-shoot versions, the mere presence of a useable viewfinder is a tremendous advantage. Viewfinders help stabilize the camera against the eyebrow, and they offer a significant advantage while shooting in bright sunshine, allowing the scene to be seen clearly and the composition to be framed precisely. Putting a DSLR viewfinder to your eye cuts out everything except what you will see in your shot, and sometimes even more.

The T7 adheres to the EOS Rebel heritage of employing a pentamirror rather than a pentaprism for the viewfinder. With more air-to-glass surface transitions, a pentamirror viewfinder is not as brilliant. However, it is lighter and less expensive.

Metering System

Similar to the Rebel T5 and T6, the Rebel T7's viewfinder houses Canon's 63-zone dual-layer light sensor. The camera can calculate exposures more precisely by taking into account color and brightness in addition to the amount of light entering the camera.

The metering system of the T6 was quite effective. Evaluative metering (linkable to all AF points), Partial metering (about 10% of viewfinder at center), and Center-weighted average metering are accessible, although spot metering is conspicuously lacking. The metering range of EV 1 to EV 20 is acceptable for typical use but inadequate in very low light conditions.

The T6's auto-white balance functioned admirably, and EOS cameras are renowned for their ability to capture vivid colors.

Autofocus

The focusing technology is another concession taken to reduce the T7's price tag. DSLRs in the Canon EOS Rebel Series include Canon's entry-level AF technology. While not the fastest, Canon's entry-level phase detection AF is far faster than the contrast-detection AF available in many point-and-shoot cameras and smartphone cameras.

The Rebel T7 inherited the AF system of the Rebel T3 for its AF system. This 9-point AF system features a high-precision, f/5.6 cross-type central point (sensitive to lines of contrast in two directions as opposed to one) surrounded by 8 AF points placed in a diamond pattern. All EOS Rebel DSLRs require a lens with a maximum aperture of f/5.6 or wider (as indicated by the lens) for AF to function. This includes all autofocus lenses currently on the market, although some lens + extender combinations will not enable autofocus.

This AF system has a working range of EV 0 to 18 for the central AF point and EV 1 to 18 for the remaining AF points.

In One-Shot AF mode, the T6 and, by extension, the T7, provide exceptionally consistent and precise focusing. AI Servo AF mode, in which the camera is instructed to predict the point of focus at the time of shutter release while following a moving target, is significantly more difficult for a camera.

While the T7 offers contrast AF in Live View mode, it is excruciatingly sluggish when compared to the quick phase-detection AF speeds of DSLRs or the Dual Pixel AF employed in many of Canon's most recent EOS models.

Extra Characteristics

The Rebel T6's established Wi-Fi & NFC capability was arguably the most significant upgrade over the

Rebel T5, and the T7 features the same capabilities. Using the free Canon Camera Connect app, Wi-Fi and NFC facilitate the transfer of photos and videos to compatible mobile devices through Wi-Fi and NFC. This app has a great deal of development potential. Wi-Fi also supports wireless printing remotely to a suitable printer.

The camera's built-in NFC (Near Field Communication) provides for quick and easy pairing with an Android handset or other NFC-capable devices, such as the Canon Connect Station CS100 video and photo storage and sharing device.

Remember that the Rebel T7 lacks a sensor self-cleaning function. Notably, this camera lacks the mirror lockup function, necessitating the use of Live View for mirror lockup functionality.

Flash

As with previous Rebel models, the T7 is equipped with a built-in flash. Not so noticeable is the fact that the T6/T7 flash is only rated at 9.2 GN (compared to the T7i's rating of 13.1 GN). Even though this flash can offer some fill light and serve as the primary light in close circumstances, it will not effectively illuminate a large area in total darkness.

It is also crucial to note that, unlike the T7i, the T7 does not include an Integrated Speedlight Transmitter. Canon flashes that are remotely controlled require an external flash controller. Similar to the Rebel T7i, the T7 has a maximum X-Sync flash shutter speed of 1/200 second.

Note that, unlike the majority of EOS cameras, the T7's hot-shoe lacks a central contact. Especially with third-party accessories, this can be problematic.

Battery

The Canon EOS Rebel T7 utilizes the same battery as the Rebel T6, T5, and T3 models: the compact and lightweight Canon LP-E10 Li-ION battery pack. The accompanying LC-E10 wall charger is compact and directly wall-plugs in (no wires).

The rating for the T7's battery life is comparable to that of the T6 and T5. However, the T7 is rated for around 500 shots.

Canon's normal ratings can frequently be surpassed, but a second/spare battery occupies minimal space and adds minimal weight to the bag with twice as many photos as feasible.

On the rear LCD, the T7 displays four levels of battery charge.

Performance

The image quality of the EOS 2000D is excellent for a camera at this price point and is a significant improvement over the 18MP sensor employed in Canon's cheap DSLRs until very recently. Canon has shaved quite a few corners in the EOS 2000D's hardware to achieve this price, but it is not apparent in the photographs.

Nevertheless, the sluggish autofocus and poor quality of the included kit lens detract from the generally pleasant handling of this camera. To get something with a better lens and better features, you have to move up the Canon range and pay more. This makes it hard for buyers to decide if the Rebel T7/EOS 2000D is enough.

CHAPTER TWO

Set Up your Device

How to use the USB device to connect it to the Computer

Before connecting the Canon Rebel t7 to a computer, it is important to understand that you will not be able to transfer images using the Wi-Fi/NFC mode. The necessary equipment is not included in the package.

Make use of a high-speed USB cable, as transferring high-resolution data with a normal cord may take too long. A USB cable with a data transfer rate of 480 Mbps should suffice.

1. Check that your Canon Rebel T7 is fully charged

The pair charger will power your camera directly, protecting the battery. It provides direct, uninterruptible electricity from the outlet.

Power off your Canon Rebel T7, remove the battery, plug in the coupler, and connect it to your computer. There is no fear of running out of battery during the transfer, and the reduced battery usage will increase its life.

Connect the Canon Rebel T7 digital camera to the computer. Make sure your Canon EOS Rebel T7 is fully charged before transferring files to your computer. This is the first and most crucial step.

If your Canon EOS Rebel T7 battery dies while downloading files, the images may be lost permanently.

It may take too long to transfer high-resolution photographs and movies without a high-speed USB cable, given their size.

2. Be patient and allow your computer to finish booting up

Turn on your computer and give it sufficient time to load into its typical routine. Before connecting the Canon EOS Rebel T7 to a computer, let all starting software load and then refresh it a few times.

3. Turn off the WiFi on the Canon Rebel T7

Now, with the camera in hand, navigate to the main menu > Wi-Fi/NFC settings. Ensure that Wi-Fi and NFC are turned off. This is important because file transfer is turned off by default when the Wi-Fi/NFC feature of the Canon EOS Rebel T7 vlogging camera is turned on.

4. Connect the USB cable

After disabling Wi-Fi and NFC on the camera, shut down the Canon EOS Rebel T7. Now, grab the USB cord and place the smaller plug into the camera's USB port and the bigger plug into your computer's USB port.

The USB port of your Canon EOS Rebel T7 is concealed beneath the rubber door that is placed on the left side of the screen.

5. Activate the camera

Now, activate the camera. If the Canon EOS utility window does not appear automatically after turning on the camera, you may need to manually start it from the software that came with the camera.

6. Begin transferring

Now that your computer is connected to the Canon vlogging camera EOS Rebel T7, you will see an option on your computer screen that says "Select and download photographs from your camera."

7. Select the destination folder.

Now scroll through the folders and choose the photographs you wish to download. To select an image, check the corresponding boxes and then click the download button.

You will then be prompted to choose a destination folder. You can either create a new folder or choose an existing one to keep your photographs in.

The Canon EOS Rebel T7 is now one of the greatest cameras available on the market.

The Canon EOS Rebel T7/2000D is loaded with features that are distinctive in their own right.

When you select the Canon flip-screen EOS Rebel T7, you will receive several features with this DSLR camera, which can naturally produce some magnificent images.

You should be aware that one of the most talked-about features of the Canon EOS Rebel T7 is its ability to transmit images instantly from the gadget to your computer.

How to connect Wi-Fi to send images

Connect your camera to your device and transmit photographs for the first time by following these steps.

After the initial connection is made, things operate a bit differently; more on this issue and NFC

connectivity will follow the steps.

1. Open **Setup Menu 3** on the camera and select **Wi-Fi Function**, which is directly below the Wi-Fi/NFC option. The subsequent screen contains four icons.

2. Select the phone icon (the second icon in the top row) and press the "Set" button.

From now on, you can choose between Easy Connection and Selecting a Network from the Connection Method screen.

3. Select **Easy Connection**, then press **Set** to highlight OK, followed **by Set again.**

On the resulting display, the camera will display the moniker you specified. You also notice a nine-character encryption key that serves as the password for your camera's Wi-Fi network.

4. Turn on Wi-Fi on your smartphone or tablet, then navigate to the wireless settings screen.

The moniker of your camera should be displayed on the list of accessible Wi-Fi networks. If no nickname was specified, the camera's name should begin with EOST7, followed by further characters.

5. Choose the camera from the list of available networks, and when asked for a password, enter the encryption key shown on the camera monitor.

After inputting the password, the smart device should be instructed to join the network.

6. Exit the settings screen on your smartphone or tablet and launch **the Canon Camera Connect app**.

If everything works out, a screen should show up on your device telling you that a new camera has been found and asking you to choose it to finish the connection.

7. Select the Canon EOS Rebel T7 camera.

8. Press the **camera's DISP button** to show which photos you want to look at.

You can choose all images, images from the past few days, images with a specified rating, or a range of file numbers. If you select anything other than All Images, you can then configure file selection settings.

9. After selecting the image format you wish to view, press the "Set" button to exit the camera's menus.

The display goes dark, and the app indicates that the camera has been connected. The home screen for the iOS version of the program is shown on the left. The same options are available on an Android device, but they look different.

10. Select **Images on camera** on your mobile device.

Your photographs are shown as thumbnails, as shown on the right.

To view images stored on the camera's memory card, hit Images on Camera (left) in the Canon Camera Connect app (right).

Hint: Tap the **I icon** in the lower-left corner of the screen to toggle between the display shown in the illustration and one that contains some shooting data for each image.

11. Tap **Select** to transfer multiple photographs.

On the left, you'll notice circles next to each thumbnail. To select an image for transfer, tap its thumbnail to mark the circle with a checkmark. Then, tap the Download icon, as seen in the image. You are prompted to decide whether you wish to email the image in its original size or reduced size, as depicted on the figure's right. To copy the photos to your device, press the option you want and then tap OK.

12. To send a single picture, go back to the main thumbnail screen, tap the photo's thumbnail, and then tap the **Download icon.**

Select the download size once more, and then tap **OK**.

After choosing the photos you want to send, click the Download icon (left) and then choose the file size (right) for local storage.

Here are a few additional pieces of the puzzle that may be of assistance:

- By pressing the Settings icon after reaching the thumbnails screen, you can modify several features of the file transfer.

- Depending on how your device's image storage is configured, the location of the image files will vary. To resolve this, look for the

Canon Camera Connect app in your device's main settings menu. You may need to grant the app permission to access the device's photo storage folder.

- For NFC transfer, locate the camera's NFC gizmo on the camera's left side, immediately in front of the door that conceals the connection ports. Figure 10-25 identifies where the NFC connection resides. Bring the device's NFC antenna into contact with the mark until the camera's display indicates that a connection has been made. Then, separate the two devices. The Camera Connect icon should then instantly launch on the device.

- Whenever a Wi-Fi connection is active, the lamp identified on the figure's right-side illuminates. While the devices are linked, you can't use the camera's controls to get to the camera's features.

How to remove Battery and Memory Card

1. First and foremost, set the power to off.

- Open the cover

- Ensure the access lamp is turned off before opening the cover.

- If [recording] appears, close the lid or cover.

2. Disconnect the battery.

  - Get rid of the battery from the device by depressing the battery lock lever as indicated by the arrow.

  - Be sure to connect the included protective cover to the battery to prevent electrical contacts from short-circuiting.

3. Take the card away.

- Gently insert the card, then release it to eject it.

- Pull the card out straight.

4. Close the lid or cover.

- Apply pressure until the cover snaps shut.

How the Battery can be Charged

Two official chargers exist.

- LC-E10 is directly wall-mounted. The prongs are folded out and linked to the charger.

- The LC-E10E includes a power cord. However, it is typically difficult to locate in retailers.

The two are switching chargers, so they can be used in other countries with voltages ranging from 100V to 240V. However, you may still require an international adaptor when traveling abroad (depending on which countries you're visiting; I'm speaking to a regular plug adapter).

Again, there are numerous aftermarket alternatives. They can provide three benefits:

- They can be significantly less expensive. They are frequently supplied with batteries, giving them an extremely good deal.

- Several are dual battery chargers, which can simultaneously charge two batteries.

- Some can be charged via a USB power source, allowing for greater flexibility when traveling or charging on location.

As with aftermarket batteries (and other aftermarket electronics), the quality control of no-name brands might vary.

Externally Energizing a Canon Rebel T7 with AC Power

Using an ACK-E10 AC adapter and DC Coupler Kit, you can run your Rebel T7 off of external AC power.

These accessories are not included with the camera, so you must purchase them separately.

There are also far less expensive aftermarket alternatives.

These are frequently marketed in various configurations. Some kits offer everything necessary to get started. However, you can also purchase the parts separately if you wish (or if those are more readily available at your preferred camera retailer). Typically, you will need a CA-PS7000 AC Adapter and a DR-E10 DC Coupler to operate your T7 from AC power.

CHAPTER THREE

The Process of Mounting the Lens

If your camera does not already have a lens attached to it, choose the lens you want to use and then loosen (but do not completely remove) the cover on the back lens. In most cases, the lens that you intend to attach vertically should be stored in a section of your camera bag designated specifically for that purpose. In this way, the lens will be protected from any potential mishaps and will be easily accessible. If you release the screw on the back of the lens cap, you will be able to remove it from the back of the lens at the very last possible minute, therefore protecting the rear lens element until that time.

After that, remove the body cover by rotating it so that it faces the button that releases the shutter. Always attach the body cover to the camera while there is no lens attached to it. This will help prevent dust from entering the interior of the camera, where it could potentially accumulate on the mirror, focusing screen, and inner mirror box, and could even make its way past the shutter and onto the sensor. In addition, the body cover safeguards the mirror from damage caused by extraneous things, such as your fingers, if you are not cautious enough to handle it properly.

After the body cap has been removed, remove the rear lens cap from the lens and set it to the side for later use. Install the lens onto the camera by lining up the alignment indicator on the lens barrel (which should be colored red for EF lenses and colored white for EF-S lenses) with the corresponding red or white dot on the camera's lens mount.

To properly secure the lens, rotate it counterclockwise away from the shutter button until it clicks into place. Put the focus mode switch on the lens into the AF position (autofocus). If the lens hood is bayoneted onto the lens in the incorrect position (which makes the lens and hood combination more portable), twist it off and remount it with the edge facing in the other direction.

The front element of the lens is protected by a lens hood from accidental bumps, stray fingerprints, and flare caused by light entering the lens from beyond the frame.

How to Modify Diopter Correction

People who have a vision that isn't perfect might perhaps get some advantages from using the viewfinder's optical correction features. It's possible that your contact lenses or glasses already provide enough correction, but if you wear glasses and want to use the EOS Rebel T7 without them, you may make use of the built-in diopter adjustment on the camera, which ranges from −3 to +1 and can be set as you need it to be.

When you are ready to take a picture, give the shutter release button a half push to illuminate the arrows in the viewfinder. Next, adjust the dioptric adjustment knob that is located next to the viewfinder until the arrows seem clear when you look through the viewfinder.

If the correction that is already present in the viewfinder window is not sufficient, Canon offers ten additional corrective lenses from the Dioptric Adjustment Lens Series E. If many people use your camera and each needs a different diopter setting, you can save time by keeping track of the number of clicks and direction (clockwise to raise the diopter power; counterclockwise to lower the diopter value) required to go from one user to another. This will allow you to adjust the diopter setting appropriately for each person. It should be brought to your attention that there are a total of 18 detents.

How to Turn the Camera On and Off

This On/Off switch of the camera can be found on the right shoulder, and it is clearly labeled with the words On and Off, as well as a symbol that looks like a movie camera. Do not flip the switch beyond the On position to the Movie setting unless you want to record movies.

Simply turning the camera on will get it ready for usage, provided that you have already installed a lens, replaced the battery, and inserted a memory card. You can start taking pictures right away if you turn the Mode Dial (which is located to the left of the On/Off button) to either the P (Program mode) or the green A+ (Scene Intelligent Auto mode) designations.

How to adjust the Time and Date Settings

When you turn the camera on by moving the On/Off button on the top of the device to the On position, the sensor will be cleaned immediately (unless you expressly deactivate this function). The camera will remain on or in standby mode until you switch it off manually. To save the life of the battery, the camera goes into sleep mode after thirty seconds of being idle.

Simply pressing the button that releases the shutter will restart the feature. The automatic sensor cleaning operation is not activated when the standby state is exited; it remains off. The very first time you use the camera, you could get a message asking you to enter the time and date. (It's possible that this information was programmed into your camera by a third party before it was sold to you.) Simply adhere to these directions by pressing the appropriate directional buttons:

1. Press the **MENU button**.

2. Turn the **Main Dial** in the direction indicated to bring up the Function Settings menu. Tap the tab, and then touch the **SET button** on the touch screen.

3. Using the up and down arrows, choose the **Date/Time/Zone input**, and then press the **SET button**, which is located in the center of the keypad to the right of the LCD.

4. On the screen that follows, use the directional buttons to scroll down until you reach the date/time item. Once the desired format for the month, day, year, hour, minute, or second is highlighted in the gold box (using a 24-hour clock), you can activate that value by pressing the **OK/SET button**. Take note that, just above the number, there will be shown a pair of triangles that point in opposite directions, up and down.

5. To raise or decrease the value, use the up and down arrow keys on your keyboard. Press the **OK/SET button** to verify the value that you have input.

6. Proceed to activate or disable **Daylight Saving Time** and adjust the time zone (a list of the major city that represents each time Zone, such as New York, Chicago, Denver, and Los Angeles). If the time zone that is now selected does not correspond to where you are, you may change it by using the up and down arrows to choose the appropriate city, then clicking the **SET/OK button**.

7. Choose either the **OK button** (if you are satisfied with the adjustments you made) or the **Cancel button** (to return to the menu page without making any changes). To confirm your option, tap the **SET/OK button**.

8. After altering the date and time, tap the **MENU button** to close it.

CHAPTER FOUR

How to Insert a Secure Digital Memory Card

In the Shooting 1 menu, there is an option called Release Shutter without Card that allows you to activate or disable the camera's shutter release capabilities when there is no memory card attached to the device. Consequently, the last step is to put a memory card into the device. To remove the cover, slide the door located on the right side of the body of the camera toward the back of the device. You should only remove the memory card after the camera has been switched off; however, the camera will inform you if you open the door while it is still writing pictures to the memory card.

When inserting the memory card, make sure that the label is at the back of the camera and that the edge that bears the connection is facing the slot.

The pre-flight checklist is considered complete after the door has been shut. When the time comes in the future for you to remove the memory card, press it inward to cause it to pop out of its slot.

Exploring the Camera's External Feature

If you are new to digital single-lens reflex photography, you may find that some aspects of using your camera, such as interacting with the lens, are unclear. Even if you have experience with digital single-lens reflex cameras, it is still a good idea to spend some time becoming familiar with the controls of a new camera before taking your first picture with it.

- **Top controls**

The top of the camera is where you should begin investigating the various external controls available on the camera. The following is a guide to the many different parts and components that can be found in that area, beginning at the upper-right corner and proceeding clockwise:

1. **Red-eye reduction/Self-timer lamp:** This lamp produces a brief burst of light before the real flash when your flash is set to the Red-Eye Reduction mode. The hypothesis proposes that the pupils of your participants would constrict in response to the light, hence lowering the risk of their developing red eyes. If the self-timer feature of the camera is engaged, the light will turn on during the countdown that occurs just before the shutter is released.

2. **The shutter button:** The function of the shutter button is probably already obvious to you at this point. Nevertheless, you may be unaware that taking a photo while utilizing autofocus and auto-exposure necessitates two more steps: After you have pressed the shutter

button halfway and waited for the camera to correct the focus and exposure, you can complete shooting the image by pressing the shutter button all the way. You will be surprised at how many people mess up their images by hitting the button too rapidly, preventing the camera from making adjustments to the exposure and focus settings. The camera may make a beeping sound to let you know that it has successfully focused and is now ready to take the photo.

3. **Main dial:** This dial allows the user to make adjustments to a variety of camera settings. Even though this dial performs such an important role, it just goes by the label **"Main dial."**

4. **Flash button:** When using one of the more complex exposure settings, you may turn on the built-in flash by pressing this button (P, Tv, Av, and M).

5. **The On/Off switch:** This control does exactly what its name suggests it would do. Be aware, however, that even if the switch is set to the On position, the camera will still enter sleep mode after 30 seconds of inactivity to save battery life. You can change this time by accessing Setup Menu 1 and selecting the Auto Power Off option.

6. **Mode dial:** When taking still images, you may select to have the camera operate in either a fully automated, semi-automatic, or manual exposure mode by using the mode dial. Rotate the dial to choose an exposure mode. To activate the movie mode, rotate the dial until it is aligned with the corresponding sign on the screen.

7. **Viewfinder diopter adjustment dial:** Dial for dioptric adjustment of the viewfinder: Turning

this dial will allow you to adjust the focus of the viewfinder to suit your eyes.

8. **Flash hot shoe:** This is the connection point for external flashes and other accessories, such as the GP-E2 GPS receiver.

9. **Focal plane indicator:** It displays the plane at which the light from the camera's lens is focused onto the image sensor. It is only relevant if you need to record the exact distance between your subject and the camera like you would if you were working in forensics, and only if you need to record that distance. If you want a more accurate reading, you should base the subject distance measurement on this mark rather than the end of the lens or another point on the camera body. This will allow you to get a more accurate reading.

10.   **The speaker:** When you play a movie that has audio, the sound travels via these very small holes.

- **Controls located on the back of the camera (back of the body control)**

Moving from the top of the camera to the back of it will lead you to a buffet of controls like the ones that are listed below. *Note:* The buttons with a white icon are used to execute tasks in the shooting mode, while the buttons with blue icons are used to perform operations in the playback mode.

Since some buttons come in two different colors, it is possible to use them for any of the aforementioned functions.

1. **The AF Point Selection/Magnify button:** When you are in specific shooting modes, pressing this button allows you to choose which of the camera's autofocus points you wish to be used when the camera is focusing. When you

are in playback mode, pressing this button causes the image to be shown at a larger size (as indicated by the plus sign within the magnifying glass icon that represents the button).

2. **The AE Lock/Index/Reduce button:** This button allows you to lock the autoexposure (AE) settings as well as the flash exposure while you are taking pictures (FE). In addition, clicking this button enables you to view photos in two different ways: first, it switches the display mode of the screen to the Index mode, which allows you to view the thumbnails of multiple images all at once; second, it reduces the amount of magnification applied to each image as it is displayed individually.

3. Pressing the button labeled **"Live View/Movie-record"** will put the camera into the **"Live View"** mode, which enables you to arrange your shots by looking at the LCD rather than

via the viewfinder. During the process of creating a movie, you can also use this button to start and stop the recording.

4. **The Exposure Compensation/Erase button:** When the camera is set to the P, Tv, or Av exposure mode, you can change the exposure compensation by pressing this button and turning the Main dial. This is a function that allows you to instruct the camera to take a picture that is either brighter or darker the next time it is used. If you are utilizing the M exposure mode, you may change the aperture by pressing the button and turning the Main dial (f-stop). You can delete images while they are being played back by pressing this button; the blue trash can icon represents **"dump it"** because it stands for **"delete it."**

5. Pressing the **Q (Quick Control) button** will bring up the Quick Control button, which is one way

to adjust the picture settings. When you hit this button, the Quick Control window will open.

6. The **DISP button** lets you change the way pictures are displayed in Live View, Movie, and Playback modes. When there are available customization options, pressing this button will bring up the Camera Settings display.

7. **Set button and cross keys:** Four buttons surround the Set button and are referred to as cross keys. These buttons, when used in conjunction with one another, may complete a variety of activities, including the selection of settings from the camera's menus. After using the cross keys to navigate through the menus, press the **Set button** when you are ready to choose an item from one of the menus. In viewfinder photography, which is when you frame your shots by looking through the viewfinder rather than the display, the

cross keys also serve particular roles, which are denoted by the labels on the cross keys themselves:

- Press the **up-arrow key** on your keyboard to change the ISO setting. This exposure-related parameter determines how sensitive the camera is to light in the scene being captured. You are only able to make adjustments to this setting while using the P, Tv, Av, or M exposure modes. (If you touch this cross key or any other keys when the Mode dial is set to one of those settings and nothing happens, press and hold the shutter button halfway, and then release it, to wake up the camera.)

- You can change the AF mode by hitting the **right cross key** on your keyboard. This option allows you to alter the behavior of the camera when it comes to focusing on subjects. Once again, you will only be able to view this setting if you are shooting in the P, Tv, Av, or M mode.

- Press the **left cross key** to change to another drive mode. Using the options for the Drive mode, you can change the camera's shooting mode from single-frame shooting to continuous recording, or to shooting with a self-timer or remote control.

- Press the down **cross key** to make changes to the **White Balance**. You have the option of adjusting the white balance to ensure that colors are shown accurately. In addition, you will not be able to utilize the White Balance option until the Mode slider is set to either the P, Tv, Av, or M position.

- It is important to keep in mind that the cross keys are used for activities connected to autofocusing while the camera is in Live View or when it is making a video.

8. **Play back button:** Pressing this button will place the camera into the picture-review mode.

9. **Menu button**: Pressing this button will bring up the menu options for the camera.

10.   **Wi-Fi indicator:** if this light is on, it means that a connection to the wireless network is active.

11.   **Card access light:** When the camera is writing data to the memory card, the card access light will light up. If the light is on, you should refrain from turning off the camera or removing the memory card to reduce the likelihood of causing damage to the device.

Front-left Control Features

There are three important features placed on the front left side of the camera, and they are as follows:

1. **Lens-release button:** By pressing this button, you may remove the lens from the camera and free it from its attachment. To remove the lens from the camera, press and hold the shutter button while turning the lens so that it faces the side of the camera.

2. **Microphone:** This cluster of holes is what connects to the microphone that is attached to the camera.

3. **Near Field Communication (NFC) mark:** The Near Field Communication (NFC) mark indicates the position of the camera's signal emission, which enables it to connect wirelessly to a smartphone or tablet by using the technology of near field communication.

4. **Connection ports:** The inputs for linking the camera to other devices are hidden behind a cover that is identified as the port access door:

- **Remote-control terminal:** This is where you would attach a wired remote control, such as the Canon Remote Switch RS-60E3 model.

- **Digital terminal (USB port):** You will need to make use of this terminal to connect your camera to the USB port located on your personal computer. This will allow you to download images. If your printer supports PictBridge technology, you may also print directly from the camera by connecting the two devices via their respective USB ports and sending the print job from the camera.

- **HDMI terminal:** To enable playback on a high-definition television or screen, you can connect the camera to this terminal by using an optional HDMI male to mini-C cable. Connecting the camera to this terminal will allow you to use the HDMI terminal.

Basic Camera Features and Settings

- **Camera Menus Orders (Understanding menu basics)**

A limited number of camera settings can be adjusted by using the buttons and controls located on the camera's exterior. To access further options, use the Menu button on your keyboard.

Categories are used to organize the items on menus. The following is a breakdown of the color-coding used for the menu icons: the icon for the Shooting menu is colored red, the icon for the Playback menu is colored blue, the icon for the

Setup menu is colored gold, and the icon for My Menu is colored green.

In addition, the number of dots that are located above the icon represents the menu number. For example, there will be one dot for the Shooting Menu 1 icon, two dots for the Shooting Menu 2 symbol, and so on. An icon that is highlighted indicates the menu that is now active.

To see all the available settings, the Mode dial must be set to either P, AV, TV, or M. In other aspects of the camera's settings, where you have very little control over how it functions, you are only presented with a limited amount of customization possibilities. When you switch the camera to Movie mode, three of the four Shooting menus are replaced with Movie menus that provide you options for recording movies. Shooting Menu 1 is relocated to the right to create room for the Movie menus, and the Movie menus replace three of the four Shooting menus. To denote this change, the icon that represents the Movie menus has been updated to depict a movie camera. Additionally, the My Menu icon is not displayed in Movie mode.

To navigate through the menus, either turn the Main dial or use the left or right cross key on the keyboard. After arriving at a menu, you may highlight the feature you desire to update by pressing the up or down cross key on your keyboard. After you have selected the Set button, the options will be shown to you. After making your selection using the arrow keys, confirm your choice by pressing the Set button once again. When you are ready to exit the menus, you may start shooting by hitting the shutter button halfway before releasing it or pressing the Menu button instead.

CHAPTER FIVE

How to Navigate the Custom Function Screens

Only in the P, Tv, Av, and M exposure modes can you reach Setup Menu 3, and when you do so, you can access the submenus with more options by selecting Custom Functions. This menu can only be accessible in the P, Tv, Av, and M exposure modes.

Check out the following settings:

1. When it comes to custom functions, there are four categories to choose from: exposure, picture, autofocus/drive, and operation/others. In the upper-left corner of the screen, the category name and number are shown. Additionally, the selected function's number is shown in the upper-right corner of the window.

2. The configuration options for the currently selected function are presented in the middle of the screen: The blue lettering indicates the current setting for the device. The default configuration is denoted by the number 0, which stands for **"default."**

3. The current configurations of all Custom Functions are represented by numbers that may be found at the very bottom of the screen: The numbers in the top row represent the Custom Functions, and a thin horizontal bar located just above each number indicates which of the available functions is now active. The bottom row displays, for each Custom Function, the number that corresponds to the setting that is now in effect; once again, 0 serves as the default value.

4. To go from one Custom Function to the next, you need to press the left or right cross key

depending on which direction you want to go. After you have located the adjustment that you want, you can make it by pressing the **Set button**. After an update, the highlight box that is centered on the currently used option will display on the screen. You can confirm your choice by using the arrow keys to move the highlight box over the option you want to choose and then pressing the **Set button** a second time to confirm your option. You can exit the menu and continue shooting by either pressing and holding the shutter button for a short period and then releasing it, just as you would with a conventional menu display.

How to Display the Camera Settings

Screen

When the menus are open, pressing the DISP button will bring up the Camera Settings screen for you to configure the camera.

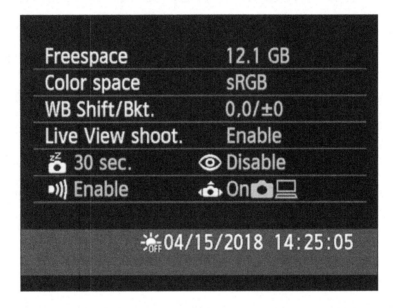

When the Mode dial is turned, various settings and information are shown before the user. When using the active exposure mode, all parameters that cannot be altered will be hidden from view on the screen. The following, in order from the top to the bottom of the screen, is your decoder ring:

1. **Freespace:** This indicates how much space is currently available for use when saving data on the memory card of your camera.

2. **Color System:** This setting shows whether the camera's color space is set to sRGB or Adobe RGB. (Since you won't have time to look at that information just yet, you should stay with sRGB.)

3. **White Balance Shift and Bracketing:** It explains the amount of White Balance shift or bracketing that is present.

4. **Live View Shooting:** This function alerts you to the current status of Live View.

5. The **Red-Eye Reduction flash mode and the Auto Power Off flash mode** are two of the

options that are located on the same line on the screen. The first reading on Setup Menu 1 provides you the delay time selected for the Auto Power Off option, and the second symbol on Shooting Menu 1 tells you whether or not the flash is set to Red-Eye Reduction mode. Both of these readouts are located on the first page of the first menu.

6. Toggle the sound on and off using the Shooting Menu 1 option, and the first choice gives you control over whether or not the camera beeps after specific operations. The auto-rotate display is also accessible via this menu. When you play back videos or view photographs on your computer, the **"Auto Rotate" option** on the **"Setup Menu 1"** determines whether or not the visuals are rotated to the appropriate orientation automatically.

7. **Date and Time:** The date and time are shown on the very last line of the display. You can change these values by selecting the "Date/Time/Zone" option from the **"Setup"** menu. The sun icon at the top of the line indicates whether or not you told the camera to automatically adjust the time to reflect Daylight Saving Time (DST) based on whether or not you asked the camera to do so. You can, of course, check the status of an option simply by navigating to the menu that contains it. The only exception to this rule is the value associated with the amount of free card space. You don't have to travel through any menus to check out a number of the crucial features that are shown on the Camera Settings display.

8. To exit the Camera Settings panel, either press and hold the **Menu button** or partially push and then release the shutter button.

How to Use the Monitor as Viewfinder in

Live View Shooting

When working in Live View, you can choose to compose your shots using the screen rather than the viewfinder on your camera. When recording videos, you will not be able to use the viewfinder; instead, you will have to rely only on the display. How you activate Live View determines whether you will be able to shoot still photographs or video:

1. **Live View for still photography:** Before beginning, ensure that the menus support Live View shooting and that it is turned on. You can customize how the Mode dial is set up, which determines where the option will be located. You may access it via Scene Intelligent Auto, Creative Auto, and Scene modes through the Shooting Menu 2 on your camera. In the P, Tv, Av, and M shooting modes, you can find the Live View option on the fourth page of the

Shooting Menu. Since it's easy to hit the Live View button and switch to Live View when you don't want to, the menu choice should preferably be set to Disable. This is because it's simple to press the Live View button by accident. After enabling the feature in the menu, you may access Live View by pressing the button on the camera's back. A clicking sound is produced by the internal mirror of the camera, which is designed to flip up to transfer the image captured by the lens to the viewfinder. After that point, you will no longer be able to see anything in the viewfinder since whatever was in front of the lens will now be shown on the screen. Data representing the different camera settings are presented over the live image in the viewfinder. By hitting the **DISP button**, you will be able to modify the kind of data that is shown. Simply pressing the Live View button once again will exit the Live View mode, allowing you to return to utilizing the viewfinder instead.

2. **Live view for recording movies:** Rotate the Mode dial to the Movie mode icon to utilize Live View to capture movies. You can begin and stop recording by tapping the Live View button when the feature is active in the camera. To exit movie mode, rotate the Setting dial until you reach one of the other exposure modes.

Although taking images through a viewfinder is relatively comparable to taking pictures in live view, some important features, like autofocusing, function quite differently in live view than they do in the viewfinder.

Adjusting the Shooting Settings Display

When you turn on the camera, the display turns on automatically and stays on for the first thirty seconds thereafter until you manually turn it off. The display may be restarted if the shutter button is pressed until it clicks, and then the button is released. Before the display turns off by itself, you can turn it off manually by pressing the DISP button.

When you look at the Shooting Settings display, you will see that some of the options have curved arrows around them. These arrows indicate that you can alter the setting by rotating the Main dial. For example, in the shutter-priority autoexposure mode (Tv on the Mode dial), the shutter speed is bordered by the arrows, suggesting that the setting is active and that rotating the Main dial will affect the value. This is because the value is dependent on the shutter speed.

Viewfinder data reading

When you first turn on the camera, all the relevant information appears at the bottom of the viewfinder. After displaying this data, it immediately turns off to save the life of the battery. To turn on the display, press and hold the shutter button until it is halfway depressed, and then let go. The little markings in the middle of the viewfinder serve as a representation of the auto-focusing locations.

Another important point to remember about a subject in the viewfinder is that it shows the maximum number of burst frames, which is something that is frequently missed by photographers. This applies to photography in continuous capture mode, in which the camera swiftly takes off several photographs as long as the shutter button is depressed. Even though the viewfinder can only display a maximum of nine images at a time, the actual number of frames captured in a burst may be more. You shouldn't pay attention to it till the number starts to decline near 0, which indicates that the camera's memory buffer (its temporary internal data-storage tank) is filled up. In other words, you shouldn't pay attention to it until the number starts to decrease toward 0. If the problem persists, be sure to give the camera some time to catch up with your finger on the shutter button.

CHAPTER SIX

How to Change the Live View Display

When you are in Live View mode, you can use the DISP button to change the amount of data and the kind of data that is shown on the screen. Again, the data that is presented will be different depending on whether or not you are shooting static shots or moving pictures. In Movie mode, the histogram display will not be displayed, and some data will alter to give options for recording movies rather than still photographs.

A histogram is a useful tool that may be used in the process of determining exposure. However, take in mind that when you use flash, the histogram will become less prominent since the final exposure will contain light from the flash in addition to the light from the ambient light. Additionally, the shutter speed Bulb, which can only be accessed via the M

(Manual) exposure mode, is responsible for a reduction in the size of the histogram.

In bulb mode, the shutter will remain open for as long as the button on the shutter's control ring is depressed. Because the camera is unable to predict how long you will continue to press and hold that button, it is unable to generate a histogram that will appropriately depict the exposure you have chosen.

In the case that the camera overheats to the point that it has to turn off to protect itself from further harm, a thermometer will appear in the live view. Additional customization options are available for the Live View display, including the following:

1. **Display an alignment grid:** The camera may display a grid on the screen to assist you with the composition of your shots. There are two distinct options for the grid's layout to choose from. The location at which you activate the grid will be determined by the exposure setting you are using. In the P, Tv, Av, or M

modes, the choice may be found on the fourth page of the Shooting Menu. The Shooting Menu 2 is a mode for taking still photographs. When you are in Movie mode, look for the option on Movie Menu 2.

2. **Modify the time of the exposure-data countdown timing:** By default, if you don't hit any camera buttons for 8 seconds, exposure data like f-stop and shutter speed disappear from the display. You can alter the shutdown time so that the exposure data is shown for a longer period while you are shooting in the P, Tv, Av, or M exposure mode. On Shooting Menu 4, under the category of "Still Photography," you'll find the Metering Timer option. The exact option may be found on Movie Menu 2 in Movie Mode. Given that the metering device operates off of battery power, the cutoff time needs to be as brief as is practically practicable.

How to Use the Quick Control Screen to modify settings

As its name indicates, the Quick Control panel provides a manner that is both quick and easy to modify a number of the camera's settings. Any exposure mode may have its settings altered using this screen, but which options are accessible depends depend on the mode you pick and whether you're employing the viewfinder or Live View mode for still photography.

In addition, the settings for the Quick Control switch around depending on whether or not the camera is in the shooting mode or the playback mode. When taking pictures via the viewfinder on a camera that is not configured to shoot in Live View, the following steps must be followed to use the Quick Control panel:

1. **To return to shooting mode if a menu screen is shown, use the Menu button:** Although a menu is shown, it is not possible to access the Quick Settings panel at this time. Depending on the settings for the camera, the display may either show you the Shooting Settings screen or it may go completely black.

2. **Make a selection by pressing the Q button:** This will put you in the Quick Control mode, which will highlight one of the options that are shown on the screen. If nothing happens when you hit the shutter button, you need to give it a half-press and then let go of it to startle the camera awake and get it ready to take a picture. If there is no activity, the camera may be in sleep mode.

3. **Using the cross keys, highlight the option you want to alter:** It is important to take notice that when you have highlighted a setting for the first time, a text suggestion will show that

describes the purpose of the setting. If you find the text tips to be annoying, you can turn them off by disabling the Feature Guide option found on the Setup Menu 2 screen.

4. Select the option that you would want to take: You might try any of the following approaches:

- Turn the Main dial to go through the list of possible choices in the menu. The current setting is shown at the very bottom of the screen. The icon of a little wheel that can be seen in the top-right corner of the text bar acts as a visual reminder to use the Main dial for this function.

- To see all the potential configurations, click the **Set button**. For instance, if you are altering the White Balance setting and you press the **Set button**, you will see a display on the screen. You can highlight the option that you want to choose by either spinning the Main dial or using the cross keys on the keyboard. Sometimes, regardless of whether or not the Feature Guide is active, the screen will display a summary or remark about the option that is being selected.

• Once you have made your choice, press the **Set button** so that you are brought back to the Quick Control screen.

5. Exit Quick Control mode by pressing the **Q button** a second time to bring up the main shooting menu. Additionally, you have the option of pressing the shutter button halfway before releasing it. In either scenario, you are required to return to the **Shooting Settings** window.

Note that the only change is that in Live View and Movie modes, after hitting the Q button, the options appear on the left side of the screen. This is the only difference. Once again, the choice that is now being used will be in bold; take attention to the orange line that surrounds the AWB (White Balance). Take notice that the information on your current setting may be found at the very bottom of the screen.

In addition, you have the option of rotating the Main dial to cycle among the different settings or pressing the Set button to see all the choices at the same time. You can now see the DISP label that was previously hidden behind the settings.

Basic Setup Options Overview

You can customize the Canon Rebel T7/2000D to suit your specific needs as a photographer, which is just one of the many advantages that come with making that investment. The parts that follow will go through many different setup options, some of which you may be considering right this second.

- **Setup Menu 1**

You can get the following options by using Setup Menu 1:

1. **Auto Power Off:** To save the life of the battery, the camera will power off by itself after a certain period of inactivity. By default, the shutdown will take place after thirty seconds; however, you have the option of changing the delay to one, two, four, or fifteen minutes. You also have the option to entirely disable auto shutdown by selecting the option labeled **"Disable."** However, even if you do this, the monitor will still turn off on its own if you ignore the camera for more than half an hour. Simply pressing the Menu, DISP, Playback, or Live View keys or swiftly half-pressing and releasing the shutter button is all that is required to bring the display back to life.

2. **File Numbering:** This option sets the names that the camera assigns to your picture files, and it can be found in the menu.

- **Continuous** is the default setting; your files are consecutively numbered from 0001 to 9999, and all of your photographs are automatically saved in the same folder (100Canon) unless you choose to save them in a different location using the Select Folder option, which is discussed in the following bullet point. Even if you use a different memory card, the order of the numbers will stay the same.

- **Auto Reset:** If you select this option, the camera will start numbering files again at 0001 whenever you add a new memory card or create a new folder, regardless of whether you select this option or not.

- **Manual Reset:** Select this option if you want the camera to begin a new numbering sequence for your next shot at 0001 and you will be responsible for doing it manually. Your newly created files are immediately saved in a fresh folder for you. After that, the mode that you were using before—either Continuous or Auto Reset—will be restored on the camera so that you may continue to number the images you take.

3. **Select a Folder:** Your camera will automatically create a 100Canon folder for initial file storage and insert up to 9,999 images in the folder. You have the option to change this setting. When you reach picture 9999, the camera creates a new folder on the memory card that is labeled 101Canon to store the subsequent 9,999 images. When you reset the file numbers on the camera using the manual controls, a new folder will also be produced. If

your memory card has more than one folder, you will need to use the option labeled **"Select Folder"** to choose the folder on the card where you want to save the images you take in the future. But clicking the menu option also brings up a handy feature: You are never restricted from creating new storage folders at any time. For instance, you may decide to create separate files for each person who uses the camera.

Identifying which folder is now visible and selecting a different folder can be done as follows:

- **Verify the status of the currently selected folder:** When you pick **Select Folder** to see a list of all folders, the currently selected folder will be printed in blue font and highlighted when the list is shown. If you count the number that is shown to the right of the folder's name, you will be able to determine how many photographs are included inside the folder. You can see a thumbnail view of the first and last photos in the folder, in addition to the file IDs for those photographs.

- **Choose another folder to look in:** After you have selected the folder using the arrow keys, choose it by pressing the **Set button**.

- **Screen color:** This menu gives you the option of customizing the Shooting Settings display by selecting one of four different color schemes.

Setup Menu 2

You will find these options on the second page of the Setup Menu:

1. **LCD Brightness:** You can change the level of brightness shown on the camera's LCD screen by using this option. If you want to continue, keep in mind that the exposure that appears on the display may not be the case. The

default setting of the brightness scale is **"4"**, which is located in the middle of the scale.

2. **LCD Off/On Btn:** You can direct the camera to display the Shooting Settings screen when you push the shutter button halfway by choosing this option and then pressing the LCD Off/On Btn. You can do one of the following:

- **Shutter Btn:** The display turns off when you only push the shutter button halfway; when you press it all the way, it turns back on. This is the setup that is used by default.

- **Shutter/DISP:** When you press the shutter button halfway, the display turns off and remains off even after you let go of the button. This occurs regardless of whether or not you continue to hold it down. After you have touched the DISP button, the Shooting Settings screen will show up on the screen.

- **Display Stays On:** The display will continue to be active until you hit the DISP button. This setting is a waste of battery life since it keeps the monitor on even while your eye is focused on the viewfinder of the camera.

3. **Day/Time/Zone:** When you power on your camera for the first time, it will automatically offer you this choice and ask you to choose the date, time, and time zone. In addition, you have the option of deciding whether or not you would want the clock to adjust itself automatically for Daylight Saving Time (accomplish this by selecting the little sun symbol and then choosing On or Off).

4. **Language:** Using this option, you can choose the language that will be used for any text that shows on the monitor of the camera.

5. **Clean Manually:** Selecting this option will lock the camera mirror, allowing you to clean the

image sensor by hand. This option can be made only when the Mode dial is positioned in the P, TV, or AV positions.

6. **Function Guide:** When you enable this option and choose particular camera settings, the monitor will display notes that explain the feature. Initially, the feature guide windows will be helpful; but, as you get more familiar with your camera, you will find that having them continuously appear can be a nuisance.

7. **GPS Device Settings:** This menu item allows the user to configure the GP-E2 GPS device, which may be used but is not required.

Setup Menu 3

For access to all the options on this menu, the Mode dial must be set to P, Tv, Av, or M. Only the first two choices on the menu pertain to the camera's wireless technology. An overview of what Setup Menu 3 has to offer is provided below:

1. **Wi-Fi/NFC:** This option lets you toggle the camera's wireless connection on or off. To extend the life of the battery, turn the feature off when not in use.

2. **Wi-Fi function:** When the Wi-Fi/NFC option is enabled, this feature enables you to change a variety of aspects of how the camera connects wirelessly with your smartphone or tablet.

3. **Certification Logo Display:** On this screen, only a handful of the certifications that the camera claims to have obtained from the electronics industry are shown by logos.

4. **Custom Functions:** Click on this link to learn more about a variety of complex choices.

5. **Copyright information:** If you want to add your copyright information to the metadata (hidden extra data) of your picture files, start by selecting this menu option.

6. **Clear Settings:** Choose this option to return to the default shooting settings. After selecting the option, choose **Clear All Camera Settings** to reset all settings apart from Custom Functions. Choose **Clear All Custom Functions** as an alternative to going back to the default settings.

How to Select an Exposure Mode

The first thing to think about while taking photos is the exposure mode, which is chosen via the Mode dial.

The Basic Zone and the Creative Zone are the two different types of exposure modes available for still photography. Your decision affects how much control you have over the shutter speed and aperture, two key exposure settings, as well as several other options, including those relating to color and flash photography.

Your choice does not impact your focusing choices, even though it affects your access to exposure and color settings as well as other advanced camera features. If your lens supports autofocus, you may choose between manual and autofocus in any setting. Access to features that alter how the focusing mechanism works is restricted in Creative Zone modes.

CHAPTER SEVEN

Basic Zone Modes

The following point-and-shoot modes are available in this zone, and the associated icons are shown on the Mode dial:

1. The most basic option is **Scene Intelligent Auto**, in which the camera examines the scene and selects the settings it thinks would best capture the subject.

2. **Flash Off:** Comparable to Scene Intelligent Auto, but with the flash turned off.

3. **Creative Auto:** With the inclusion of user override options, this mode is comparable to Scene Intelligent Auto. You can exercise some creative control by changing some

picture properties, including whether the background is blurry.

4. This option refers to exposure settings that are more commonly known as scene modes as **Image Zone modes**. Each mode in this group is designed to capture certain types of occurrences.

You have the following options to choose from:

- Portrait, for capturing portraits as usual with a sharp subject and a blurred background
- Landscape, for capturing stunning panoramas or other items across a large area while maintaining sharp focus at a wide distance.
- Close-up, emphasizes the subject by blurring the background while shooting flowers and other close-up objects.
- Sports, for taking pictures of moving objects (whether they happen to be playing a sport or not)

- Food was created to produce stunning, especially vivid images of that delectable food you're about to enjoy and want to share on Facebook or Instagram before you do.
- Night Portrait, for better midnight individual flash photography outside.

Creative Zone Modes

When you're ready to have more control over the camera, go up to one of these settings: Aperture-priority autoexposure, shutter-priority autoexposure, programmable autoexposure, and M (manual exposure). Remember that these settings collectively referred to as advanced exposure modes, provide you access to all of your camera's menu options as well as all exposure settings.

How to Choose a Shutter-Release (Drive) Mode

Drive mode is the setting that tells the camera what to do when you press the shutter button: Record one frame, a series of frames, or one or more shots after a short pause. In other words, this setting regulates when and how the shutter is opened to expose the picture.

Understanding the Drive Mode Options

There are a total of five Drive mode options for your camera. However, access to all five is only possible if the Mode dial is set to one of the complex exposure settings (P, Tv, Av, or M). In the other settings, your choices are more limited.

The Drive modes and which ones can be used with each exposure mode are covered in detail below:

1. **Single mode:** Use this option as the default shooting mode. It is indicated by the single

square in the margin above: The camera only records one frame for every press of the shutter button. Single mode is the default setting for all exposure modes, except for Portrait and Sports, which restrict using Single mode and instead favor Continuous mode, which is detailed below. To shoot only one picture in each of those two modes, choose one of the Self-Timer Drive mode settings.

2. **Continuous (burst) mode:** Continuous mode, also known as burst mode, takes a series of pictures as long as the shutter button is down. It is symbolized by the **"many frames"** symbol in the margin. The camera is capable of recording three frames per second. Keep the following in mind while using Continuous mode:

- **Continuous mode is the default setting for Portrait and Sports modes:** Although it may seem unusual, employing continuous capture while shooting portraits may enable you to catch the perfect expression on your subject's face or, at the very least, the brief interval between blinks.

- None of the other scene modes support Continuous mode, Auto mode, or Auto Flash Off mode. If you don't want to shoot in Portrait or Sports mode, you must switch to Creative Auto, P, Tv, Av, or M exposure mode to utilize burst-style shooting.

- The number of frames per second is influenced by your shutter speed. At a sluggish shutter speed, the camera may not be able to operate at its maximum frame rate.

- The number of frames per second is decreased when flash is used. The frame rate decreases because the flash needs time to recycle between photographs.

- The burst rate is influenced by both the speed of the memory card and the picture quality level. The file size of each photograph is decided by the degree of image quality; the larger the file, the longer it will take the camera to record the photograph to the memory card. The read-write speed also affects how quickly the card can store all the picture data.

- Whether the focus is shifted between each frame depends on the AF Operation setting.

Self-timer Settings

Self-timer mode postpones the shutter release until a few seconds after you press the shutter button. Self-timer mode has traditionally been the default option for self-portraits, but you can also use it to eliminate the camera shake that may be caused by just pressing the shutter button. Mount the camera on a tripod and activate the self-timer mode to snap hands-free, and hence motion-free, photographs.

Your camera has three self-timer settings:

1. **Self-Timer:** 10 Seconds: Delays the shutter release by 10 seconds.

2. **Self-Timer: 2 Second:** This option, which is only accessible in the P, Tv, Av, and M exposure settings, opens the shutter two seconds after you press the shutter button.

3. **Self-Timer:** Continuous: With this option selected, the camera will shoot photographs continuously for 10 seconds after you press the shutter. With each shutter release, the camera may be configured to shoot two to ten photos.

When using any of the Self-Timer settings, it's a good idea to cover the viewfinder. If not, light may penetrate the viewfinder and affect the camera's calculations for exposure.

How to Check and Modify the Drive Mode

The current Drive mode choice would often be represented by a symbol on the Shooting Settings and Live View screens. The Drive mode icon will appear in a different place depending on your exposure setting.

How you change the Drive mode depends on whether you're framing the photo with Live View or the viewfinder:

The steps:

1. Press the left cross key to begin (not available in Live View mode). To aid in remembering what they do, two of the Drive mode icons have been put on the key. The settings screen seen in the picture displays after tapping the cross key. To choose how many continuous

photographs you want the Self-Timer Continuous mode to shoot, press the up or down cross key.

2. **Use the Quick Control screen:** After pressing the Q button to open Quick Control mode, choose the **Drive mode icon**. The name of the current setting is shown at the bottom of the screen. Turn the Main dial to cycle through the different options; press Set to see the selection screen. You must use this method to change the Drive mode while Live View is enabled; during Live View shooting, pressing the left cross key changes the focus.

Setting the Image Quality Setting

The current Image Quality level is often represented by a symbol on the Shooting Settings and Live View displays. Your exposure mode determines the options you have for adjusting the Image Quality setting.

1. **Shooting Menu 1 (any exposure mode):** Click the **Set button** after selecting the Image Quality option to examine the different settings.

2. **Quick Control screen (available only in P, TV, AV, and M modes):** After choosing a setting, turn the Main dial to cycle through the others. You might also press the Set button to see all options at once.

The picture settings options include the following:

1. Three pieces of information are displayed at the top of the Shooting Menu's Image Quality selection screen: the resolution, or total pixel count (measured in megapixels), the pixel dimensions (number of horizontal pixels followed by the number of vertical pixels), and the number of additional shots that can be stored on the current memory card with

the current Image Quality setting. The same information appears at the bottom of the Quick Control screen when the Image Quality option is selected.

2. The menu's following two rows of icons represent the potential Image Quality selections as follows: The S2 and S3 settings, as well as the arc-marked settings, all take pictures in the JPEG file format. The JPEG compression level, which affects the picture quality and file size, is represented by the arc symbols. There are two options: Fine and Normal.

3. There are five resolution possibilities within the JPEG category, identified by the letters L, M, S1, S2, and S3 (large, medium, small, smaller, smallest).

4. Another option is to take photos in Raw format. The greatest pixel count is always

achieved when producing raw files at a Large resolution level. One of the two Raw settings also records a JPEG Fine version of the image with high quality.

5. The Optimum Image Quality option that is ideal for you will depend on a variety of factors, including how you want to use your images and how much time you want to spend on your computer editing them.

CHAPTER EIGHT

Using the Camera Flash

How to Add Flash

The built-in flash on your camera is an easy and practical way to add light to a dim environment. The exposure mode, as described in more detail in the following sections, determines whether flash may be used and what flash capabilities are accessible.

Take into account the following advice before moving forward:

1. The ISO setting and lens focal length affect the built-in flash's range: The ISO level affects how sensitive the camera is to light. The flash range at an 18mm lens focal length, which is the widest angle on the 18-55mm kit lens, is around 3 to 8.5 feet at the lowest ISO setting (ISO 100). The flash range of this lens is about

3 to 5 feet at its maximum focal length (55mm). Use an external flash that is stronger than the camera's built-in flash or a higher ISO setting to illuminate a distant subject.

2. **Refrain from approaching too closely:** If the flash is too near to the subject, the illumination may not be complete. So, take a test shot and modify your shooting distance as necessary.

3. **Watch out for shadows cast by the lens or lens hood:** When using a long lens, the flashlight may strike the lens, creating unwanted shadows. The same is true with a lens hood.

4. **The flash recycles while a "Busy" signal is displayed:** The flash is on when there is a lightning bolt in the viewfinder. The lightning bolt and the word "Busy" together suggest that the flash needs a few seconds to recharge. The Busy alert could also show up on the screen when recording in Live View

mode. For flash photography with bright backgrounds, use a slower shutter speed.

5. The camera has more time to capture ambient light with a slow shutter speed, requiring less flash to illuminate the subject. The flashlight that lights your subject is thus softer, while background objects outside of the flash's range are brighter. While most cameras include a slow-sync flash setting, the T7/2000D just requires you to choose the required slow shutter speed. To control the shutter speed, turn the Mode dial to Tv (shutter-priority) or M (manual). By rotating the Main dial, you may change the shutter speed. There are shutter speeds up to 30 seconds. Setting the Mode dial to Night Portrait will automatically use a slower shutter speed than other flash-enabled modes, which is ideal if you want slow-shutter flash effects but are not yet comfortable with Tv or M mode. Keep in mind that if the subject or camera moves

while the exposure is being made, a slow shutter speed might cause a blur. Use a tripod as a result, and tell your subject to maintain the greatest level of steadiness.

6. The fastest shutter speed you may use with the built-in flash is 1/200 second. This restriction occurs because the camera has to time the flash firing with the opening of the shutter. Two problems might arise as a consequence of the shutter speed limitation. First, at 1/200 second, a moving object could seem fuzzy. Additionally, a faster shutter speed is necessary for very bright conditions to avoid overexposure.

How to Enable and Disable Flash

You can be able to use the flash or manage its firing depending on the exposure setting.

Here is the current situation:

1. **Scene Intelligent Auto, Portrait, Close-Up, and Night Portrait**: If the camera decides that extra light is needed, it will raise and fire the flash automatically. The flash will remain closed if you don't.

2. **Landscape, Sports, and Flash Off modes:** The flash is often turned off in these settings.

3. **Food mode:** By default, the flash is turned off, and Canon advises against using it in this mode to prevent distracting shadows and reflections on the surfaces of plates, cutlery, and glasses. However, if you decide to use the flash, you may modify it as needed using the Quick Control interface. (The icons for the Creative Auto mode and those for the flash On and Off settings are the same.) Half-pressing the shutter button triggers the internal flash when the flash is enabled.

4. There are three flash modes available: Creative Auto, Auto, and Manual.

- **Auto Flash:** The camera chooses when to use the flash depending on the amount of light in the immediate area.

- **On:** The flash fires regardless of the level of ambient lighting. A great method for lighting the faces of individuals in bright situations is the fill flash.

- **Off:** Under no circumstances, even if it has been raised since the last shot, does the flash ignite.

- Press the **Q button** to bring up the **Quick Control panel** and choose the flash mode from there. To switch between the three flash modes, turn the **Main dial** after selecting the flash option with the cross keys. Alternatively, you can press the **Set button** to see a menu with all the available flash settings.

5. **The modes P, Tv, Av, and M:** To use the built-in flash, press the Flash button on the camera's top. The button is situated between the Main dial and the Mode dial on the upper right side of the camera. The flash will activate when the button is pushed and take your next photo. To turn off the flash, just close the flash unit. There is no such thing as an auto flash in these exposure settings, but don't worry—you may manually control whether or not flash is used in your photographs. Shutter speed has some bearing on your flash effects.

Additionally, depending on which of the following four exposure modes you choose, there are several ranges of acceptable shutter speeds for flash photography:

- The camera selects a shutter speed between 1/60 and 1/200 of a second in the Food mode and P mode.

- In Av mode, the camera automatically selects a shutter speed between 1/200 and 30 seconds while using flash. By using Custom Function 3, Flash Sync Speed in Av Mode, you may raise the slow limit of this range to reduce camera blurry moving objects that may be caused by a slow shutter. The range of 1/200 to 30 seconds is used by default option Auto (option 0 on the menu screen). While the shutter speed at setting 2 is always 1/200 second, it varies between 1/200 and 1/60 second at setting 1.

- In TV mode, choose a shutter speed that ranges from 1/200 to 30 seconds. Always use a tripod and tell your subject to remain steady while utilizing a slow shutter speed to avoid blurry pictures.

- **M mode:** With one more option, this offers access to the same range as TV mode: But as long as the shutter button is down, the bulb maintains the shutter open. By default, the flash starts firing at the start of the exposure. Additionally, if an external flash is connected, you can choose to have the flash fire just after the exposure rather than at the start and finish. To change this component of the flash, choose **Shutter Sync**.

How to Use Flash with Red-Eye Reduction

When a subject's retinas reflect the flashlight in the camera lens, red-eye results. Humans only experience red eyes; in animals, the reflected light is often yellow, white, or green.

If you see red-eye, try turning on the Red-Eye Reduction flash. When the shutter button is depressed halfway and focus is achieved, the Red-

Eye Reduction Lamp on the front of the camera glows. The goal of this light is to make the subject's pupils smaller, which lowers the amount of light entering the eye and, therefore, the possibility of red eye. The flash will start when you fully press the shutter button.

Any exposure setting that allows flash may have this capability activated. It may be found on Shooting Menu 1. It should be noted that the camera does not display any symbols to denote that the Red-Eye Reduction mode is on in the viewfinder, on the Shooting Settings, or the Live View displays.

The exposure index at the bottom of the viewfinder display is replaced by a row of vertical bars after halfway pushing the shutter button in Red-Eye Reduction flash mode. The bars quickly veer away from the edge and go toward the middle. Wait until all the bars are gone before shooting a picture for the best effects. The subject's pupils have time to constrict in response to the red-eye reduction lamp during the wait. This feature is not available in Live

View mode, only while taking pictures via the viewfinder.

How to Modify Flash Power with Flash Exposure Compensation

You could sometimes like a little bit more or a little bit less light than the camera deems ideal. If so, you can use Flash Exposure Compensation to change the flash's output.

Exposure value (EV) values are used to indicate the parameters for flash exposure compensation. When the setting is EV 0.0, there is no flash adjustment; nevertheless, the flash intensity may be changed to EV +2.0 or EV -2.0. You could sometimes find it necessary to increase the flash power, but don't anticipate the built-in flash to perform miracles at +2.0 Flash Exposure Compensation. Any built-in flash has a limited range, thus it can't light up far away objects.

The following techniques can be used to modify flash power:

1. **Quick Control display:** This is by far the easiest method to take (not displayed in Live View mode). After moving to the Quick Control display, highlight the Flash Exposure Compensation amount. (Note that unless Flash Exposure Compensation has already been adjusted, this value does not appear until you engage the Quick Control panel.) To modify the strength of the flash, turn the Main dial. Alternatively, you can press the **Set button** to bring up the second screen seen in the image, which has a meter and a warning that, if you use an external flash, the compensation you set on the flash itself trumps the setting on your camera. Use the right/left arrow keys to change this display's flash intensity. When finished, click **Set**.

2. **Menu Shooting Step 1:** From the Shooting Menu 1 menu, choose **Flash Control.** Make sure the menu that appears has the first option, Flash Firing, selected. Next, choose Built-in Flash Func Setting and press Set to display the appropriate screen, as shown in the picture. To activate the control, choose **Flash Exp Comp** and then press Set. Use the left and right cross keys to change the value after that.

The Set button may also be set up to send you directly to the Flash Exposure Compensation option. Custom Function 9 is used to make this alteration. If you often utilize Live View with flash compensation, this change may save you a ton of time since you won't need to use Shooting Menu 1 to change the flash compensation option.

The value is shown in Live View and on the Shooting Settings page when Flash Exposure Compensation is enabled. A plus/minus flash indicator is visible in the viewfinder, but the Flash Exposure

Compensation value is not. The flash sign disappears from all displays if Flash Exposure Compensation is set to 0.

Any adjustments you make to the flash power remain in effect even after the camera is off until you reset the control. Before using your flash, be sure to check the settings. Additionally, the impact produced by Flash Exposure Compensation can clash with the Auto Lighting Optimizer feature, thus it could be essential to disable it.

How to Lock the Flash Exposure

The camera produces a brief preflash before the actual flash when you press the shutter button to take a picture with the flash on. This preflash is used to determine the amount of flash power needed to expose the photo appropriately.

Since the system makes assumptions about where your subject should be in the frame, the data the camera gathers from the preflash may sometimes be off-target. Your camera has a Flash Exposure Lock, or FE Lock, feature to address this problem. You can use this tool to adjust the flash intensity so that it only affects the center of the picture.

Unfortunately, FE Lock is not accessible in Live View mode. You must turn off Live View and use the viewfinder to compose your photographs if you wish to use this feature. The steps that follow show you how to lock flash exposure. Locate the AE Lock button first before starting. (On the back of the camera, the button is in the upper-right corner.) Do not press the button yet; just rest your thumb there.

Carry out the following settings:

1. With the flash on, position the subject of the photo such that it is inside the area of focus. If you do not want the subject to be in the center of the finished image, you can reframe the picture after locking the flash exposure.

2. The camera measures the scene's illumination by partly pressing the shutter button. The

autofocus system will function if you choose autofocus, however for now you may ignore this option. You may modify the final focusing distance after measuring the flash exposure.

3. After releasing the shutter button, wait one second before pressing the AE Lock button. This causes the camera to fire a preflash and display the letters FEL in the viewfinder. (The term "FEL" stands for flash exposure lock.) The asterisk that appears next to the flash indication in the viewfinder is likewise shown adjacent to the AE Lock button on the camera body. Around 16 seconds will pass during the flash's active period.

4. If required, reframe the photo to get the ideal arrangement.

5. To set the focus when in autofocus mode, partly press and hold the shutter button. Turn

the focusing ring on the lens to focus in manual focus mode.

Another benefit of using flash exposure lock while taking portrait photos is. Sometimes the preflash causes people to blink, which means their eyes are closed at the same moment of exposure when the actual flash and exposure happen shortly after the preflash. You may use the flash exposure lock to fire the preflash and then wait a few seconds for the subject's eyes to adjust before snapping the actual picture.

Additionally, because the flash exposure option is in effect for roughly 16 seconds, you can snap several shots without using a preflash by using the same flash exposure setting. The number of images that may be taken in 16 seconds varies, but the flash must have time to recycle between shots.

CHAPTER NINE

How to Scene Intelligent Auto Mode

Set the camera on Scene Intelligent Auto for the simplest camera operation; if you're shooting without a flash, choose **Flash Off**. The only difference between this mode and Scene Intelligent Auto is that, as the name implies, no flash will be used.

The term **"Scene Intelligent Auto"** refers to how the camera analyzes the scenario using its digital brain since, after all, it is an intelligent camera. The camera then selects the best settings for that scene.

The bulk of photo-taking chores are handled by the camera in both modes, but there are a few decisions to be made, such as whether to use the viewfinder or Live View, which shows a real-time preview of the subject on the camera monitor. Your decision will have an impact on how the camera's focusing system functions and, therefore, how you take images.

Both sets of instructions assume that the camera is being used with its default settings. To return to the factory settings, set the Mode dial to P, TV, or M, and then choose **Clear Settings** from Setup Menu 3. In all point-and-shoot modes, this menu option is not available.

Scene Intelligent Auto and Flash Off

settings for viewfinder photography

The procedures listed below show how to use the camera's default settings and focus while using the Scene Intelligent Auto or Flash Off exposure modes. Do not follow the manual focusing instructions if your lens does not autofocus when used with the T7/2000D. Instead, focus manually.

1. On the Mode dial, choose **Scene Intelligent Auto**. Alternatively. Choose **Flash Off** to take pictures without a flash.

2. Set the lens to autofocus: Turn the AF switch on the 18-55mm kit lens.

3. Using the viewfinder, position the subject such that it is in front of the focusing point. The autofocus spots are represented by the nine rectangles scattered over the viewfinder's frame. When the subject is positioned in such a way that it falls within the center autofocus point, autofocusing is often the fastest and most accurate.

4. The camera's autofocus and autoexposure meters start to work when you push and hold the shutter button halfway down. If the camera believes that additional light is necessary when in auto exposure mode, the flash will activate. Additionally, the flash may

produce an AF-assist beam, which is made up of a few short light pulses intended to help the autofocus system find the target. One or more of the autofocus points will glow red to indicate which areas of the picture are in focus when the camera focuses.

The focus indicator in the viewfinder will often light up and you will likely hear a little beep. As long as the shutter button is pressed down, the focus is locked. The focus lights in the viewfinder, however, may not light up if the camera senses movement in front of the lens, and you could hear a series of beeps. Both indications show that the camera is now in continuous autofocus, which fine-tunes focus right up until the shutter is released. In this scenario, your only duty is to keep the subject inside the range of the focusing points.

5. Keep pressing the shutter button to take the picture: After the recording process is finished, the picture briefly appears on the camera's

monitor. Click the shutter button if the picture is not visible or if you'd like to see it in greater detail.

Several further hints about the Scene Intelligent Auto and Flash Off modes:

1. **Exposure:** The camera shows the chosen exposure settings at the bottom of the viewfinder after exposure metering. You can choose to ignore all of this information but the shutter speed option. This number may flicker in low light when the camera alerts you that the shutter speed could be too slow for secure handholding. Use a tripod while the shutter speed is flashing since any camera movement during the exposure might result in blurring. This issue often only arises when using Flash Off mode in dim lighting. Most people can handhold the camera while it is in Scene Intelligent Auto mode since the flash of the camera provides enough light to maintain a

quick shutter speed (although it never hurts to use a tripod just in case).

Another advantage is image stabilization, which reduces little camera trembling. Put the Stabilizer switch on the kit lens to the On position to activate this feature. If your subject moves during a long exposure, whether or not you are using a tripod, it could seem blurry. The camera's light sensitivity may also need to be improved by using a high ISO setting when there is inadequate lighting. A high ISO may unfortunately result in noise, a defect that makes the picture seem grainy.

2. **Drive mode:** By default, the camera is in Single mode, which takes one picture with each press of the shutter. Use the continuous Self-Timer mode as an option, or the standard Self-Timer mode (10-second delay) (record up to nine frames with each press of the shutter

button). Use the left cross key or the Quick Control display to change the setting.

3. **Flash:** If the built-in flash activates but the picture is still too dark, go closer to the subject. This is because the range of the built-in flash is slightly restricted. The flash in Scene Intelligent Auto mode can be changed to Red-Eye Reduction mode (via Shooting Menu 1) but it cannot be turned off. You must turn the Mode dial to the Flash Off position to turn off the flash.

Scene Intelligent Auto and Flash Off settings for Live View photography

To take a picture in Live View mode using autofocus and the presets for Scene Intelligent Auto and Auto Flash Off, follow these steps:

1. From the Mode dial, choose **Scene Intelligent Auto or Flash Off.**

2. Set the lens to autofocus: Turn the AF switch on the 18-55mm kit lens.

3. By pressing the Live View button, the scene in front of the lens is shown on the monitor while the viewfinder is put to sleep. Press **DISP** to switch between the various displays; the data that shows above the scene depends on the display mode. When you press the Live View button, Live View can become inactive if nothing happens. By pressing the **Menu button**, going to Shooting Menu 4, and selecting **Enable**, you can turn Live View Shooting back on.

4. **Focus:** The camera's default focusing option for Live View is FlexiZone-Single. With the cross keys in this mode, you may move the focus frame over your subject. To turn on autofocus,

press and hold the shutter button halfway. The focus frame becomes green and the camera beeps to let you know you have focused and are prepared to snap a picture.

5. Press the shutter button down to take the picture: Live View is interrupted briefly to display a recorded image.

6. To end the Live View preview and resume framing photos via the viewfinder, press the **Live View button**.

Exposure Trio (Aperture, Shutter Speed, and ISO)

Regardless of whether it was captured with a film camera or a digital one, all images are created by focusing light via a lens onto a light-sensitive recording medium. The image sensor, an electrically complicated component that detects the light in a scene and delivers that data to the camera's data-processing center to form an image, serves as the equivalent of the film negative in a film camera.

Together, the aperture and shutter, two obstructions between the lens and the sensor, control how much light gets into the sensor. The physical configurations of the aperture, shutter, and sensor vary depending on the camera. The aperture, shutter, and a fourth factor, ISO, together define the exposure, or what most people would call picture brightness.

The three-part exposure formula functions as follows:

1. **Aperture:** The aperture, which controls the amount of light, is a movable hole in a lens-mounted diaphragm. By altering the aperture, you can change the size of the light beam that can pass through the camera. Aperture settings, or F-stops, are identified by

the letter f followed by a number, such as f/2, f/5.6, f/16, and so on.

2. **Shutter speed (controls length of light):** The shutter, which is positioned behind the aperture, works something like, um, the window shutters. When the camera is not in use, the shutter is closed, preventing light from reaching the picture sensor. When the shutter button is depressed, the shutter briefly opens, enabling light to pass through the aperture and hit the image sensor. However, the shutter remains open while you compose in Live View mode so that your image may develop on the sensor and be shown on the monitor. When you press the shutter release when the camera is in Live View mode, the shutter first closes and then reopens for the actual exposure. Shutter speed, which is measured in seconds and is stated as 1/250 second, 1/60 second, 2 seconds, and so on, is the length of time the shutter is open. The

shutter speed is also known as the exposure time.

3. **ISO (controls light sensitivity):** ISO enables you to adjust the image sensor's sensitivity to light. It is a digital function rather than a mechanical one on the camera. The numerals ISO 100, ISO 200, ISO 400, ISO 800, and so on were used by the International Organization for Standards, a photography organization, to rank each film stock according to its light sensitivity at the time.

The image-exposure formula may be expressed in its most basic form as follows:

1. The shutter speed and aperture work together to control the quantity of light that reaches the image sensor.

2. ISO determines the degree to which the light impacts how the sensor reacts.

The difficult part of the equation is that decisions you make about things like aperture, shutter speed, and ISO affect your images in ways other than exposure.

1. The aperture affects the depth of field or the distance across which the focus seems to be acceptable and sharp.

2. The shutter speed affects whether moving objects seem blurry or sharply defined.

3. ISO has an impact on image noise.

How the Depth of Field is Also Affected by Aperture

The aperture setting, or f-stop, determines how close and how far away your point of focus, which is often your subject, will be in each direction. When the depth of field is short, your subject will seem sharper focused than the background and foreground objects; conversely, when the depth of field is long, the sharp-focus zone spreads over a greater region.

You can **"stop down the aperture,"** or reduce the aperture size, to improve the depth of field, by choosing a higher f-stop number. To help you remember the relationship between f-stop and depth of field, think of the f as the focus: Increasing the f-stop number results in a larger zone of crisp focus.

How Shutter Speed Affects Motion Blur

With a high shutter speed, motion is recorded whereas moving things seem blurry with a moderate shutter speed. The movement that occurs while the shutter is open and is recorded by the camera is what causes this phenomenon, not the actual focus point of the camera. If your photograph exhibits widespread image blur, which makes even stationary objects seem out of focus, the camera may have moved during the exposure.

When using a hand-held camera with a slower shutter speed, this is always a possibility. As the exposure duration lengthens, you must maintain camera motionlessness for a longer amount of time to avoid blur caused by camera shake.

The weight of the lens and your physical condition will both have an impact on how slow a shutter speed you can use before the camera shake becomes a problem. It will be more challenging to maintain focus the heavier the lens is. The influence of camera shake on the captured picture is increased when using a long focal length lens. You may be able to use a slower shutter speed with a 55mm lens than a 200mm lens. Last but not least, it is easier to detect little blurring from a close-up viewpoint than from a distance.

You can prevent camera shaking by mounting your camera on a tripod. Check to see whether your lens has image stabilization if you need to hold the camera by hand. This might help to lessen a little camera shake. The 18-55mm kit lens has such a feature; to use it, turn the lens's Stabilizer switch to the **On position**.

CHAPTER TEN

How ISO Affects Picture Noise

Since ISO enhances the image sensor's sensitivity to light, the chance of noise increases. Photographs taken with high ISO film often suffer from noise, which resembles film grain. Although you should always use the lowest ISO setting on your camera to get the finest image quality, there are times when the lighting conditions make this impossible.

The one-step shift from ISO 100 to ISO 200 doesn't reveal any appreciable variation in the degree of noise since, thankfully, the T7/2000D doesn't encounter substantial noise until you dial up the ISO. However, noise is more noticeable the bigger the image appears, similar to other picture faults. Additionally, noise is easier to see in images that have large areas of solid color and dark areas. Even a little amount of noise is undesirable in images that need to be of the highest quality, such as those for product catalogs or vacation shots that you want to expand to poster size.

It's crucial to realize that noise isn't necessarily brought on by a high ISO. The defect may also be brought on by a shutter speed that is too slow, such as one second or longer of exposure. As a result, when a high ISO and a long shutter speed are coupled, there will be additional noise.

Exposure Modes for Advanced Lighting (P, Tv, Av, and M)

By using the Ambience and Background Blur modes when your camera is in Creative Auto mode, you can slightly modify picture brightness and depth of field. You can only actually request a little brighter or darker exposure using the Ambience setting in the scene modes.

If the picture attributes matter to you—and you should—set the Mode dial to one of the four advanced exposure settings, P, Tv, Av, or M. Canon refers to these configurations as Creative Zones in the official language.

Recounting the differences between the four modes:

1. **P (programmed autoexposure):** The camera selects the aperture and shutter speed to get a good exposure using the current ISO level. However, you may choose from a range of combinations of the two for more creative flexibility (which is why this mode is sometimes referred to generically as flexibly programmed autoexposure).

2. **Tv (shutter-priority autoexposure):** You choose a shutter speed, and the camera chooses an aperture setting that yields a respectable

exposure at that shutter speed and the active ISO setting.

3. **Av (aperture-priority autoexposure):** In this mode, the aperture setting—hence Av—for the aperture value is your choice. The opposite of shutter-priority autoexposure is this. The camera then selects the appropriate shutter speed to adequately expose the picture, again based on the ISO setting that was selected.

4. **M (manual exposure):** You can choose the aperture and shutter speed in this mode.

The first three modes are semiautomatic settings that support exposure while allowing you considerable artistic latitude. But bear in mind one important point about these modes: You may still take a picture that is improperly exposed even if the camera may not be able to choose settings in difficult lighting conditions that would provide good exposure.

Although there are no guarantees, you may be able to resolve the problem by using features like Exposure Compensation or adding flash that are designed to alter autoexposure results. When utilizing manual mode, exposure is completely within your control. However, the camera still aids you by displaying the exposure meter when you choose the M exposure setting.

How to Monitor Exposure Settings

When you press the shutter button halfway, the f-stop, shutter speed, and ISO settings are shown in the viewfinder.

In Live View mode, shutter speeds are shown as whole numbers in the viewfinder and on the monitor even when the shutter speed is set to a fraction of a second. For instance, the display just displays 50 when the shutter speed is 1/50 second.

When the shutter speed drops to 1 second or longer, the number is followed by quotation marks; for example, 1 second is represented by 1", 4 seconds is represented by 4", and so on.

Additionally, the viewfinder, Shooting Settings display, and Live View display all include an exposure meter. In the viewfinder, this graphic appears slightly different from the other two displays. Due to the narrow display area, the other two displays range from -3 to +3, while the viewfinder meter shows an exposure range of -2 to +2. If you don't know anything about exposure and the standard exposure metering technique, those numbers don't signify much right now. You should also be aware that the numbers on the meter represent exposure stops. Simply said, a stop is a term used in photography to describe an increase in exposure. You must increase exposure by one stop, which requires altering the aperture or shutter speed, to double the quantity of light that can enter the camera with the current settings. To reduce exposure by one stop, you must choose settings that permit half as much light.

The numbers on the meter indicate full stops, and the bars between them show exposure fluctuations of a third of a stop. You can change the meter such that all exposure changes are made in half-stop increments if you would like by using Custom Function 1.

Furthermore, you should be aware that the meter does several operations depending on your exposure setting, including the following:

1. The meter informs you of the suitability of your settings for M (manual) exposure mode. When the exposure indication (the bar underneath the meter), lines up with the meter's center point, the current settings will provide adequate exposure. If the indicator changes to the left of the center, toward the negative side of the scale, the camera alerts you that the image will be underexposed. If the indicator moves to the right of the center, the

image will be overexposed. The potential exposure worry grows as the signal approaches a positive or negative sign.

2. In the other exposure modes, the meter displays the current Exposure Compensation setting (P, Tv, and Av). Remember that in these exposure settings, the camera changes the shutter speed, aperture, or both to get the proper exposure. You don't need the meter to tell you if exposure is proper since it informs you whether you enabled Exposure Compensation, a feature that demands a brighter or darker exposure than the camera thinks is appropriate. When the exposure indicator is set to 0, no compensation is applied.

However, in certain lighting situations, the camera is unable to choose settings for the P, Tv, or Av modes that provide the best exposure. Since the meter in such settings shows the exposure correction amount, the camera alerts you to exposure issues as follows:

1. A blinking shutter speed number means the camera was unable to select a shutter speed that would produce an acceptable exposure at the aperture you selected in Av mode, which is mode one (aperture-priority autoexposure). Also, modify the ISO or f-stop. The camera may choose a shutter speed as slow as 30 seconds, which is enough exposure time to finish the work at almost any aperture setting. With that said, take in mind that flashing shutter speeds are unusual in Av mode. A long exposure time, however, increases the risk of blurring due to camera shake or subject movement. Unfortunately, the camera does not alert you when the shutter speed approaches a dangerous level. In conclusion, you shouldn't assume that everything is in working properly even if the

shutter speed isn't flashing in the displays. Always keep an eye on the shutter speed to make sure it remains higher than necessary for blur-free pictures.

2. **Tv mode (shutter-priority autoexposure):** The aperture value blinks to alert you when the camera cannot open or stop down the aperture enough to expose the image at the shutter speed you've selected. Either the ISO or the shutter speed can be changed.

3. **P mode (programmed autoexposure):** Both numbers blink if the camera is unable to select an aperture and shutter speed combination that properly exposes the image. You are just left with two options: change the ISO setting or the lighting. My earlier warning regarding an Av mode's slow shutter speed also applies to P mode.

How to Choose a Metering Mode for

Exposure

The metering mode determines which portion of the image is examined by the camera to determine the proper exposure. Your camera has three metering choices, which are indicated by the symbols you see in the margin on the Shooting Settings page and other displays.

You can only use all three modes at once with standard, through-the-viewfinder photography and the advanced exposure modes (P, Tv, Av, and M). In both the fully automatic exposure settings and Live View mode, the camera always uses evaluative metering.

1. **Evaluative metering:** Before selecting exposure settings that will provide a balanced exposure, the camera looks at the whole frame.

2. **Partial metering:** The exposure is only determined by the light that falls inside the center of 10% of the frame.

3. **Center-Weighted Average metering:** The camera bases exposure on each pixel, but gives the center of the image more importance or focus.

Exposure can often be accurately determined by evaluative metering. It may be jeopardized, however, if a bright background is used with a dark subject or the other way around. When the subject is very dark and the backdrop is very bright, the exposure that does the best job on the subject typically overexposes the background. You might be able to restore some of your deleted highlights by employing the Highlight Tone Priority setting. Flash can help brighten the subject without overexposing the background in outdoor photos of backlit subjects. To change the metering mode setting, choose one of the following:

1. **Quick Control screen:** Highlight the Metering mode indicator. The Main dial is used to alternate between the three settings. To view all three options on a single selection screen instead, use the **Set button**.

2. **Shooting Menu 2:** The Metering Mode option can also be found there. Be aware that regardless of whether you selected one of the other two options, the camera resets the mode to Evaluative as soon as you press **OK** to leave the settings screen, even though the camera displays this menu option while you are in Live View mode and even allows you to access the metering-mode selection screen.

The ideal approach is often to check the metering mode before each shot and choose the one that best matches your subject, frame, and lighting. But in practice, it's a hassle since you have to remember to change yet another setting in addition to the one you already need to modify. Therefore, stick with evaluative metering until you feel comfortable using all of your camera's choices. The majority of the time, it produces respectable photos, and you can always adjust the exposure settings and snap another picture if you don't like what you see on the display when you see the image. When using this option, the whole Metering mode issue is far less significant than it is when using film as a medium.

The only possible exception would be if you were capturing a series of photos with a subject and background that had drastically varied illumination. By removing the need to manually change the exposure for each photo, switching to Center-Weighted or Partial metering might thus help you save time. For instance, because their subject will nearly always be in or near the center of the frame, many portrait photographers simply use Center-Weighted or Partial metering.

CHAPTER ELEVEN

Camera Problems troubleshooting

This chapter seeks to troubleshoot these types of issues, such as why your camera won't switch on or why your battery drains so quickly. If you read on, you'll be able to return to the great outdoors whenever you feel the urge to snap some magnificent photographs.

Your DSLR camera will not power on or hold a charge

The most common cause of a camera that would not switch on is a dead or improperly installed battery. The first step is to charge your battery, followed by ensuring that it is properly fitted into the compartment.

After securing it in place, examine the dials, buttons, and memory cards. If they appear to be working and in the correct location, push the power button. If this does not work, you may need to replace the battery, or the problem may be more severe.

I've dropped my camera. What am I to do?

Start by taking a few deep breaths. There is currently nothing you can do about it. When you've stopped trembling from shock, begin inspecting each component of your camera. Check the battery compartment, memory card slots, buttons, dials, and body, as in the preceding advice.

If they appear to be in order, try the power button. Hopefully, it will begin without any problems. If nothing happens, you may want to take the camera to a camera store so they may inspect the interior.

My image quality is subpar. It appears to have spots or blotches on it

The last thing you want is to snap a flawless photograph only to discover that it is marred by dark blotches or blotchy patches. To prevent or resolve this, you must determine whether the issue is with the lens or the sensor.

You can test this by photographing a sheet of standard A4 paper with each of your lenses. Upload pictures to your computer, and if the blemishes are the same on all of them, it's your sensor.

If the marks are limited to a single type of lens, try cleaning the lens head with devices such as air blowers and specialized lens cleaning tissues; washing with an unsuitable chemical or abrasive cloth can permanently harm the lens.

My camera is unable to save photographs or videos

Most likely, there is a problem with your memory card, which may be full, corrupt, or improperly placed (generally, error messages will appear). Insert a different memory card into your camera and attempt to take photos using it. If it works, the fault is likely with your existing memory card. Note that certain cameras include a battery-saving mode that may restrict photo storage; thus, ensure that your camera is fully charged.

If so, examine the card for any anomalies. A thumbprint or a crack or scratch on the metal stripes could be the cause. Cleanse it and retry. If it's still not working, it's possible that your camera's firmware or software no longer recognizes it, so try a different card reader.

If this does not work, you should take the memory card to a camera repair shop so that they can attempt to retrieve the photographs.

My LCD monitor has stopped functioning

It may seem apparent, but many DSLR cameras can toggle the monitor on and off; therefore, you should verify that the monitor is turned on. Check your power-saving mode options at the same time. This option can abruptly power off your LCD and possibly be the cause.

Additionally, check your brightness levels. Inadvertently dimming the monitor to the point where it is nearly impossible to determine whether it is on or off can occur.

If all of these camera settings are appropriate, you should reset your camera. Most DSLR cameras require that the battery and memory card be removed for 10 minutes before being reinserted and the camera turned back on.

CONCLUSION

Even though the Rebel T7 is an entry-level camera, the image quality it produces is professional-grade, and the photographs it captures are more than adequate for many professional purposes. This camera is not nearly as feature-packed (lower build quality, fewer controls, limited options, inferior AF system, low frame rate, and small buffer depth) as well as high-performing as those typically chosen for specialist use, but there is a reason to use the T6 for professional purposes: the affordable price.

The Rebel T7 is very affordable, making it an excellent choice for humanitarian use or use in situations where camera damage is likely. Sometimes acquiring the shot is worth the cost of a camera, but if the camera is inexpensive, to begin with, the budget can be extended. Yes, a Canon EOS-1D X Mark II is more likely to endure abuse, but the 1D X II costs ten times more than the T7 and is not indestructible — nor is it difficult to steal if left unattended, such as when filming a lengthy timelapse sequence. Due to the inexpensive price of the Rebel T7, an extreme shot does not require an extreme expenditure. Set up a T7 as a photo booth for wedding and party entertainment. Mount the T7 without concern for a car, bicycle, motorcycle, boat, etc. The T7 is disposable and many backup cameras can be kept in stock at a considerable expense. Consider the importance of the photographs or films you may capture if your camera was likely to be destroyed, especially on social media.

This guide discusses everything there is to know about the Canon Rebel T7 including inserting a secure digital memory card, the controls on the camera's body, navigating the custom functions screen, how to change the live view display, and so much more.

Get into the thick of using the Canon Rebel T7 EOS 2000D in this guide and get your camera journey underway.

ABOUT THE AUTHOR

Perry Hoover is a researcher, tech Entrepreneur, blogger and a technology writer, who is fond of blogging, technology research and writing. His areas of interest include Web application penetration testing, web security/architecture, cryptography, programming languages and database security. He is well versed with the latest technology, programming languages, computer hardware/software, and programming tools. He is also an expert in database security and application security architecture and penetration testing. He loves to share information about new technology and has published dozens of articles on it.

He has written articles on different aspects of IT Technologies including IT security, data storage and application development for magazines and has also published and co-published several e-books, of which the latest is on Windows 11. He has also worked with different private agencies to provide solutions to IT problems.

69227983R00095